THE WORLD WIDE WEB

REVISED EDITION

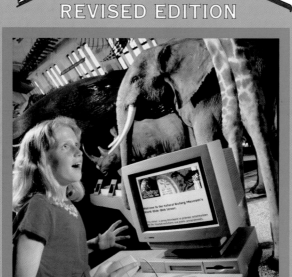

A TRUE **BOOK**

by

Larry Dane Brimner

Children's Press®

A Division of Grolier Publishing

New York London Hong Kong Sydney
Danbury, Connecticut

Reading Consultant
Linda Cornwell
Learning Resource Consultant
Indiana Department of
Education

For Mary Wong and my
friends at Desert Cove
School in Phoenix, Arizona.

Library of Congress Cataloging-in-Publication Data

Brimner, Larry Dane.
   The World Wide Web / by Larry Dane Brimner. — Rev. ed.
      p. cm. — (A true book)
   Includes bibliographical references and index.
   ISBN 0-516-21935-9 (lib.bdg.)   0-516-26856-2 (pbk.)
   1.World Wide Web —Juvenile literature. [1. World Wide Web.]
I. Title. II. Series.
TK5105.888. B76 2000
025.04—dc21   00-060385

Edited by Harold D. Underdown
   3 4 5 6 7 8 9 10 R 09 08 07 06 05 04 03

Contents

The World Wide Web is like a spider web—there are many ways to get from one place to another.

The World Wide What?

The World Wide Web is the most popular part of the Internet. Some people call it "the web" for short. In addresses it is written as WWW.

The Web got its start in Switzerland at CERN, an international particle physics lab. Scientists there had an idea. They wanted to make an easier way to share information with other scientists around the globe. Between 1989 and 1991, they developed a special computer code. They called it HTTP, or "Hypertext Transfer Protocol." HTTP made it easier to transfer information from one computer to another using the Internet. Today, everyone uses the World Wide Web to

The scientists at CERN investigate atomic particles and need to send information all over the world.

Children explore the web on their computer.

share information—scientists, teachers, parents, and kids.

How Does the Web Work?

To explore the World Wide Web, your computer will have to be hooked up to the Internet. In most cases, this means that your family will have an account with a service provider similar to America Online or Microsoft Network.

Modems (like this one) connect computers to the Internet.

For a fee, the service provider lets your computer connect or dial in to their computer, the server. In turn, the server links your computer to the Internet—the Information Superhighway.

Before your computer will be able to "talk" to the server,

though, you will need a modem or network card. They send the signals back and forth from your computer to the Internet. You will also need communications software. This will tell your modem or network card how to connect or dial in to the server.

Now all your computer needs is a web browser. With a browser, you will be ready to explore the web. Before the web was created, people had to type in complicated

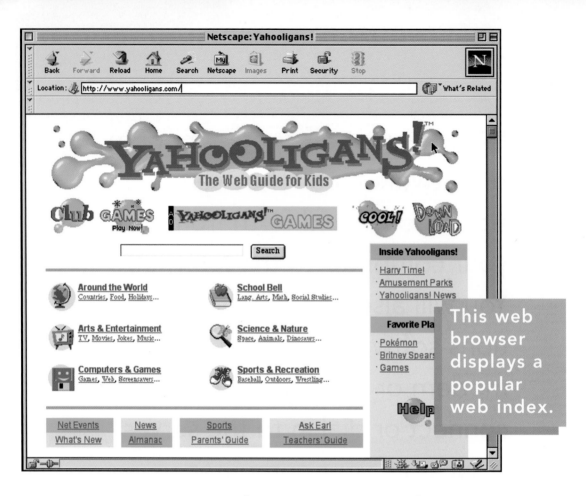

This web browser displays a popular web index.

commands to get to where they wanted to go. Browsers make things simple. In most cases, browsers let you use your mouse to get around.

Your computer becomes a travel machine! You'll be off and away to computers in other cities, countries, and continents. And you'll be looking at information (or "documents") stored on those computers.

Sights and Sounds
on the
World Wide Web

http://www.colgate.com

Colgate for Kids and Dr. Rabbit will show you how to care for your teeth.

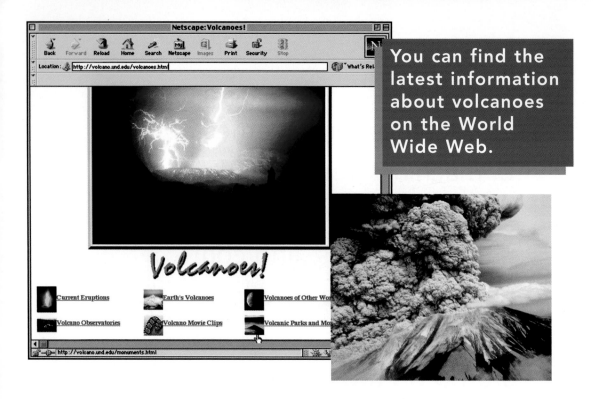

Are you a fan of *The Simpsons?* Are you writing a report on volcanoes? Are you wild about dinosaurs? The World Wide Web is loaded with documents about these and other interesting topics.

What Makes the Web Special?

Looking at documents doesn't sound very exciting, but the documents on the web are special. One of the reasons that people enjoy the web is something called "hypertext." Sometimes hypertext appears as a word or phrase displayed in a different color. Other times hypertext is underlined. The colored or underlined words are linked to different documents. These documents usually contain more information about the topic you are exploring. You can point at hypertext and click on it. When you do, your computer goes into action. You probably won't know where your computer is taking you, but—almost like

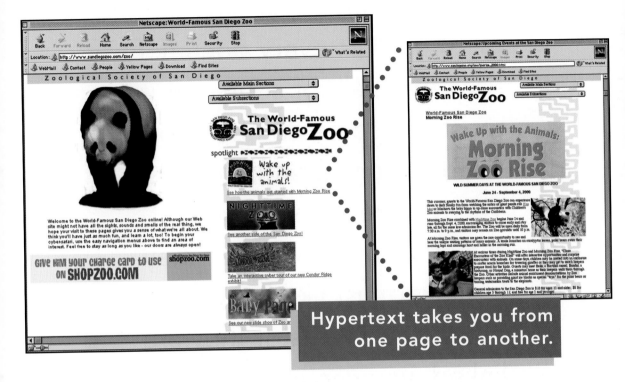

Hypertext takes you from one page to another.

magic—a new document will appear on your screen.

Another thing that makes the web so special is its use of written words, sounds, and pictures. Not every document uses them all, of course. But most use some combination of words, sounds, and pictures. The pictures may move or they may not. And they may be linked just like hypertext to other documents. If they are linked, you can click on a picture. Soon you'll be sent to another related document.

Sounds may be of anything. A lion's roar. Surf pounding

With headphones or speakers, you can listen to sounds that are included in some web pages.

the shore. A person's voice. But you won't be able to play back sound on your computer unless there is a sound card in it. Headphones or good speakers will make your listening more enjoyable.

19

HTML

Some web pages, or sites, contain a lot of color and pictures. Others sites are simple lists without much design. What makes the difference? Web pages are written using regular words, as well as a computer language called Hypertext Markup Language

(HTML). HTML is a formatting code. It tells how a page should look when it is displayed on your monitor or printed from your printer.

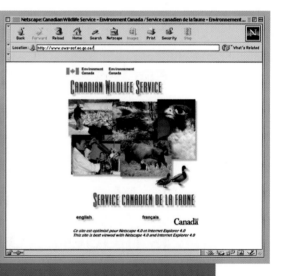

Sights and Sounds on the World Wide Web

http://www.cws-scf.ec.gc.ca/

Canadian Wildlife Service **explores the world of Canadian critters.**

When a web page is trans-
ferred to your computer, your
browser deciphers the HTML
codes. Each code means
something special. When the
page appears on your monitor, it takes its shape from the
codes. In this way, a page
appears the way its creator
intended.

Most of the time the code
is hidden from the user. If you
want to see the code, just
click on View, then on Source.

The code will appear. Here's a sample:

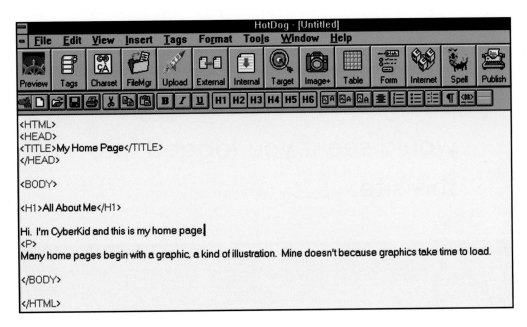

When a web browser reads the HTML code, it displays the title (My Home Page) in the title bar. The code <H1>

tells the browser to display a heading, while </H1> tells it where to end the heading. The <P> indicates a new paragraph. Here's what you would see if you logged into this site:

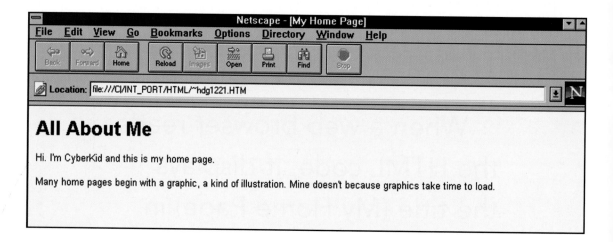

Web Addresses

An address on the World Wide Web looks like a jumble of letters. The jumble is called a URL, which stands for Uniform Resource Locator. Each site on the web has its own special URL. No two are the same. Let's say that you want to know something about the next space flight. The URL for

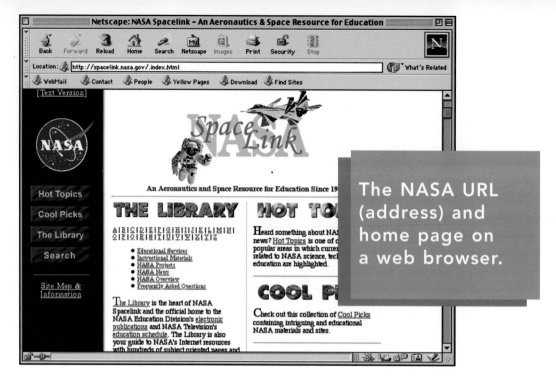

The NASA URL (address) and home page on a web browser.

NASA (the National Aeronautics and Space Administration) is

**http://spacelink.nasa.gov/.
index.html**

The prefix "http" tells you that the site is on the World Wide Web. Anything after the two slashes (//)

tells the computer where the site is located.

To begin surfing the web, type a URL into the "Location" window on your browser. Hit "Return" or "Enter." Your computer will take care of the rest. Welcome to the world of the web!

Sights and Sounds on the World Wide Web

http://forum.swarthmore. edu/dr.math/

Ask Dr. Math will help when you're stumped by math problems.

Finding Information

Imagine a library with thousands of books that are arranged in no special order. How would you ever find anything? There are thousands of sites on the World Wide Web. So far, there isn't a directory that lists them all. But there are tools that will

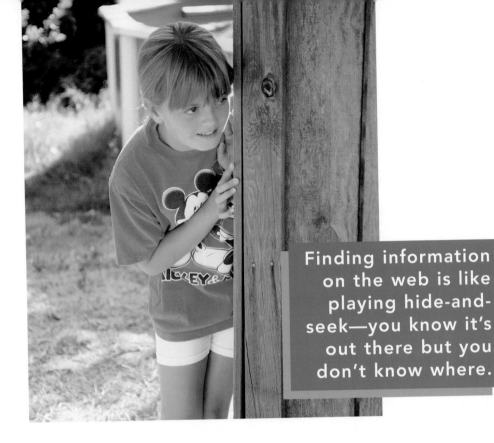

Finding information on the web is like playing hide-and-seek—you know it's out there but you don't know where.

help you zero in on the information you want. They are called search engines. Search engines let you type in key words. Then they search the web for related documents.

Two of the most popular search engine sites are AltaVista (http://www.altavista.com/) and Excite (http://www.excite.com/).

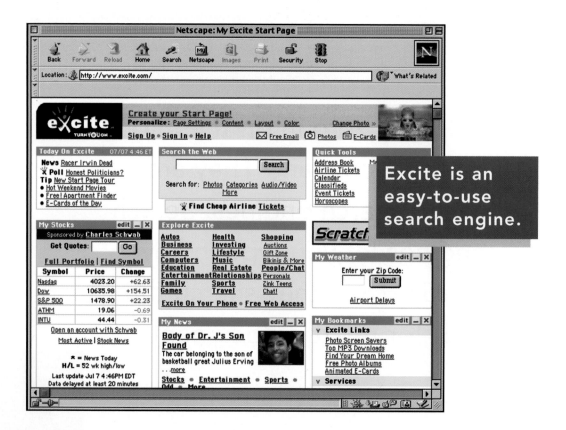

Excite is an easy-to-use search engine.

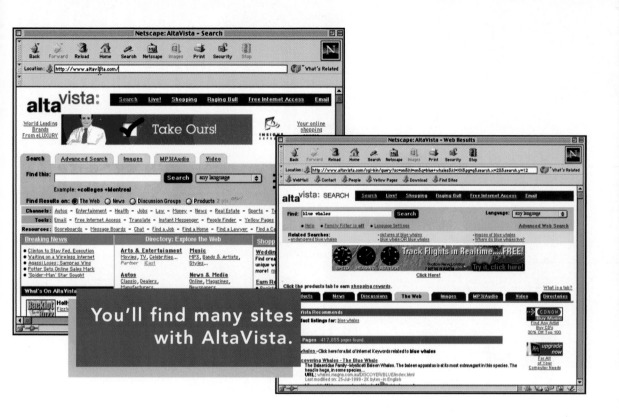

You'll find many sites with AltaVista.

Using them is a lot like using the subject guide to a library's card or electronic catalog. Simply type in some words that describe what you are looking for and click on

Finding a book may be quicker than finding the right World Wide Web site.

search. The search engine will come back with a list of sites that may cover that subject. If you don't find what you are looking for, type in some different search terms.

Sights and Sounds on the World Wide Web

http://www.ucalgary.ca/
~dkbrown/index.html

The Children's Literature Web Guide will help you stay up to date with your favorite authors.

http://www.memphis.edu/egypt/egypt.html

Color Tour of Egypt lets you explore the land of the ancient pharaohs.

Home Pages and Bookmarks

When you follow a URL to a web site, the first thing you will see is that site's home page. This is the page that welcomes you to the site. From the home page, you will be able to click on the hypertext links to other pages.

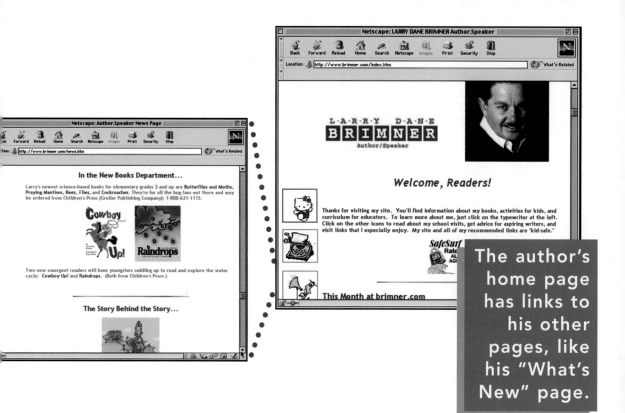

L·A·R·R·Y   D·A·N·E
BRIMNER
Author/Speaker

Welcome, Readers!

Thanks for visiting my site. You'll find information about my books, activities for kids, and curriculum for educators. To learn more about me, just click on the typewriter at the left. Click on the other icons to read about my school visits, get advice for aspiring writers, and visit links that I especially enjoy. My site and all of my recommended links are "kid-safe."

This Month at brimner.com

The author's home page has links to his other pages, like his "What's New" page.

In the New Books Department...

Larry's newest science-based books for elementary grades 3 and up are Butterflies and Moths, Praying Mantises, Bees, Flies, and Cockroaches. They're for all the bug fans out there and may be ordered from Children's Press (Grolier Publishing Company): 1-800-621-1115.

Cowboy Up!

Raindrops

Two new emergent readers will have youngsters saddling up to read and explore the water cycle: Cowboy Up! and Raindrops. (Both from Children's Press.)

The Story Behind the Story...

These are sometimes called subpages. Pages on the web are different from the pages in a book or notebook. They can be as long or as short as the site creator wants.

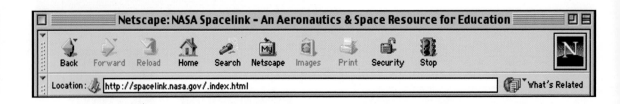

Use the "Back" button to return to pages you have already seen, the "Stop" button if you don't want to wait for a page to appear.

Most home pages have links to other URLs as well. These may be sites that are about a related topic. They may be sites the creator just finds interesting. Either way, by clicking on these links you will travel down a new path to another location on the World Wide Web.

Sometimes you will find a home page that looks interesting, but you don't have time to look at it right away. If this is the case, make a bookmark. Come back to the site when you have more

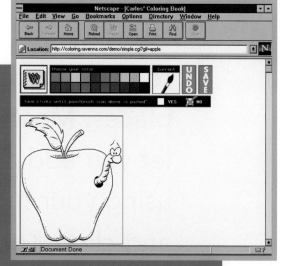

Sights and Sounds on the World Wide Web

http://www.ravenna. com/coloring/

Carlos' Coloring Book lets you become a computer artist.

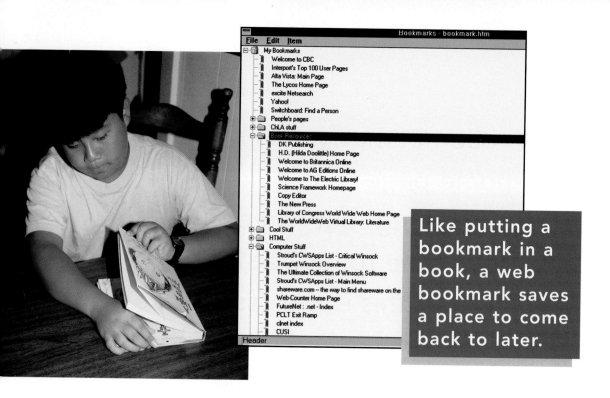

Like putting a bookmark in a book, a web bookmark saves a place to come back to later.

time. A bookmark is like a personal address book. It's a way to keep track of your favorite places. Most web browsers will let you add a bookmark by using your mouse to point-and-click. Keeping a bookmark is easier than trying to retrace your steps to a particular site. It's also easier than trying to remember a site's URL.

You will want to keep some documents. One way to do this is to use your browser's navigation buttons. Just click on "Print" to print out the information at a web site.

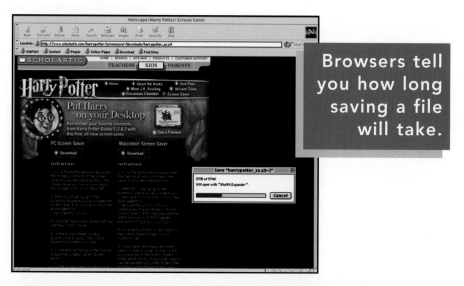

Browsers tell you how long saving a file will take.

Another way is to save the file
directly to your computer.
There is a lot of information
and software ready and waiting
on the Internet—including new
versions of web browsers!
Most of the time it can be
yours with the click of a mouse.

Sights and Sounds
on the
World Wide Web

http://www.ucmp.berkeley.
edu/diapsids/dinosaur.html

Dig into The Dinosauria page
for all your favorite dinosaurs, including T Rex.

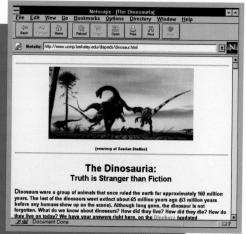

Web Safety

Some web sites are better than others. Most of them are chock full of useful information. They are interesting, fun, and even helpful. But a few sites contain nasty language and shocking photographs. Be cool and stay away from those sites.

Your teachers and parents can help. They should view this safety site before you go online:

http://www.redrival.com/ netschoolbus/

Sights and Sounds
on the
World Wide Web

http://www.safesurf.com/

Safe-surf is an organization **that approves Internet sites as safe and appropriate for kids to visit. It provides links to many kids' sites.**

Remember, anyone can put information on the web, so what you read and see may not always be true. Try to find out where the information came from before you use it.

The web can help you learn about countless topics that interest you. Use what you have learned to be a smart and safe explorer!

To Find Out More

Here are some additional resources to help you learn more about the World Wide Web:

 **Books**

 **Internet Sites**

Ahmad, Nyla. CyberSurfer: **The OWL Internet Guide for Kids.** Owl Books, 1996.

Gralla, Preston. **On-Line Kids: A Young Surfer's Guide to Cyberspace.** John Wiley & Sons, 1999.

Kazunas, Charnan and Tom. **The Internet for Kids.** Children's Press, 2000.

Mandel Family. **Cyberspace for Kids.** Instructional Fair, 1999.

Hotlist: Kids Did This!
http://sln.fi.edu/tfi/hotlists/kids.html

An index of web pages created by children.

Coolness: eZine for Kids and Teens
http://www.cybercs.com/coolness//

Chat lists, E-Pals, book recommendations for elementary-school kids around the world.

The Internet Public Library Youth Division
http://www.ipl.org/youth/

Lots of information about books and libraries. Be sure

to visit the Dr. Internet sub-page, which includes fun science and math projects, as well as a tour of the Internet designed for kids!

Earth to Kids
http://www.edf.org/ earth2kids/

A web site by the Environmental Defense Fund where you can learn about the environment. Includes games, art, poems, and books listed by age group.

Cyberkids
http://www.cyberkids.com/

Fun, games, and educational activities for kids.

Kids Only
Area on America Online that provides links to such kid-oriented areas as Highlights magazine and Nickelodeon on America Online. If you are an AOL subscriber, type keyword: kids.

Netiquette for Kids
http://www.bpl.org/www/ kids/netiquette.html

Advice on how to communicate politely on the net.

Yahooligans
http://www.yahooligans. com/

Site maintained by the web browser Yahoo that contains dozens of links to fun and educational web sites for kids.

Important Words

bookmark a personal address book of favorite web sites

home page page that welcomes a user to a World Wide Web site

hypertext a word or phrase that is linked to another World Wide Web site

hypertext markup language (HTML) formatting code that tells how a web page should look

Internet worldwide system of computers and computer networks

search engine tool that lets a user type in key words to locate related web sites

uniform resource locator (URL) an address on the World Wide Web

web browser software that lets a person use a mouse to explore the World Wide Web